Shadow

Lisa Marie Kidd

BookLeaf Publishing

Presentation by *BookLeaf Publishing*

Web: www.bookleafpub.com

E-mail: info@bookleafpub.com

ISBN: 978-93-95755-78-8

First edition 2022

DEDICATION

I dedicate this book to God,

My mom

And to those who never stopped encouraging me

Forgotten Love

I roamed the mountain
For a hero to behold the sun
You anchor my heart
And I…..

allowed your feet to go
I didn't follow or foe
I didn't cry or doubt
you new where to go...
And here ... your tomb,
I Bury you under
Nestled feet… I fell with a stranger
Darkness and fear
Looming the patches of my cradled song
hindered on bound heels
crushes my screams
while my bones drag along

And crawl In tiny dreams,
Into pockets on air
In hopes they'd soar …
and fly away from here…..

Dark Angel

She drew me in
With her soft porcelain skin
Angelic….
Like the Sight of autumn leaves
Bare before me
Petal of a rose….on my cheek

Her heat..
Melted the skin off my knees
While she climbed to the heavens
without me
And broke my beautiful dream
I was cast out..
And like a steady migration
You flew to fare away

My exposed soul froze
Awaiting for you to warm the pieces of me
You used to fly away....

Beautiful Beauty

Beauty so I rare...
I dreamed I saw it..
in the bottom of a the Dead Sea..
aligned with faces so beautiful
they blind the naked retina

Ankles broken like cracked brick
I hear hope fading
closer like a wet whip
Soulless our the lost,
we walk the streets unseen
shadows with still beating hearts
just trying to make their life
a beautiful piece
of a lucid dream

The torn winter wind
against a sharp breeze
beauty torn the deep angle
of your thorns …
 in straw like air
Here… I dangle
On the lullaby
Of a haunted song

Blooming in the dark

Promises of love
felt melting through the floors
of my home....
Dripping through the brown barked wood
You carved with hand an stone
Impenigable... I thought
While the sunlight danced
between my toes ... splatter of rocks skipped

beautifully warmth sunlight place
Un-withered... seemingly never to fade
It's facade, escaped my site
Unnerving my senses
So devastatingly wicked....
You watched....my soul
drop through my heart
while you pushed me off the edge
of my Earth
And stole the lock to my door
Where I kept it safe
Fear lingered in wait,
Volturously devouring me with anticipation...
it waits ... until this ache,
melts me....
and I succumb...

sinking into its immersive darkness
melting into this shadowy ooze,

There here weakened
you pick at me....
and erode skin from bone.
and I here lay devoured
in darkness and stone

Eternal

Ethereal presence silences me
Against a sky of pink cream
As a little girl... our love so translucent
It's as if.. it had always remained
I thought you would sprinkle the stars
And cast our love
Into an oceans heart
But fear ... here it lingers..
screams rage in ravenous torment
And her wall build around a fierce flame
to protect her beauty
so it remains....
my soul...

pouring through her feathered sky
Drapes in heavens gold
and horses that fly

Beauty in the Sea

Force fields of beauty bloom..
in light my past mourns it's extinction
Freedom is the wild wolf...daisies attatch
themselves, on the backs of beasts..
a ravaging waist land,

She feels the hunger
It's need to consume
danger fails in existence here..
Beguiled, wildly emerged
by the moments I feel I can fly
Free like the winged angels
of a black swan
You come to me in darkness,
The only radiating thing in my heart
that glows....

for I kissed a poison flower
and now my bones will cradle the sand,
and the tides will mend the sound of my tired
tear
while it floods the ocean sea
sinking into the foliage of her love

Roaring

Thunder emerges, drawing near
Laughter fills the pieces of me
The clouds drift into darkness

Emerges a frail, faint, sight of love
I remember you as a wild wind
Loving in a state of peace
Looming, breathlessly drenching
The hardened heart of yours
In shattered pieces of betrayal
You leave to foltow...

On à dim lit yellow road of stone
feel my feet submerge into the earth
Warmth of a hot white sun scorches my skin..
sounds penetrate the senses
Leaves chanting unapologetically
Reminding me…:

My home is awaiting my heart
A colour hue, of dances dreams
I stop…and merge my roots to the ground

Pierced

It grew towards me, this inanimate thing...
And I could feel the world becoming still
and I. and it.…alone
there we were... surrounded by peace.
A moment in transcendence
It remained,
complacent upon my desire for it to exist,
It never left me... or abandoned me…
Even when my emotions become just too much.
and that is what you should have been!
As opposed to water
So easily disrupted, by the fire burning
underneath it
, I just don't understand,
how you unravel love… in such a way.
that it made it ok for you.... to keep walking
away
This lifeless object, in my immediate
understanding
was capable of far more love for me... then a
man with a beating heart
I can only shrug,
and admit…that the path must keep moving
forward,

and I alone……. will be the carrier of its eternal
stride.
Your barely but a mere thought in the back of
my mind
senseless as it all seems to unstitch itself
as easily as it was built by stone...
forever in complacency
But I fear
we may always
keep walking this way

Slumber

An ethereal hunger
That penetrates me so very deeply
It unearths my desire
~ Awakens me from my slumber
Haunting images of me ravaging yoù
Curse my mind
Thrown into the depths of depravity
Let me take your hand
Allowing your fingers tips to find
Places on my body
Even the heat from the sun
Isn't allowed to find

White Willow

Oh white willow tree
How lonely In the nothing your soul must be
May I sit in the nothing with thee..
Just you and me
My iced tipped fingers,
Trace the crevices in your bark
I lean against your weeping willows
For their embrace..
May I lay upon your sleeping face
No longer in this state shall we be
For we escape the alone just you and me
Your touch it melts the cold,
from my bones
Keep me from the burden, of laying alone
I was but a fair haired maiden, by the sea
Silhouette unfolded, by a winds breeze
Now I sit, befriending.
A willow tree

Icing

He illuminates me into his gaze
Unable to hold his stare
I tremble in fear, my heart
May flutter away
Into a blue cosmic ease, the effortlessness
It takes to bring me to my knees
Beautiful as he is kind
He sweeps me into the depths of his mind
Deliciously succumbing to his
Tender embrace, alone in this moment
Inside my subconscious embrace
Devouring this red velvet cake
Icing on my tongue
I can feel my soul ache for you
Like the warmth of a shivering sun

Hidden

Here I lay
Alone within
Breathless upon
My exposed, naked skin
I only wish
To know the soul
You hide
In fear of all
The unkind eyes
As I lay in the dark
And bloom
I hear you howl
At the moon
As cold seeps through
My human skin
Your love ignited
My heart again

Freedom

Day brings the mocking of her heart.
glides across the melancholy of your lies you
helped shape my sun.
and in that rise.
shattered her sky... while you cupped my face
with your palm,
the lines wilted,
seems torn and burnt
spines peeled derived from the carving of my
shell
here it lives in ways it cannot love alone,
tormented here.... as her screams echo into a
flutter of song
Tears ... as it unravels her soul
unless though, she'll be one with me I rest upon
the nothing drifting.
Forever free

Haunted

Pouring evenecsnce of time trapped forever in
complacement softness.. it mocks the feeling
sand
Ominous strokes of body movement
I was uneasy here in this immersively grey place

Trapped between the dark and the light trapped
in a cycle of tornados torment masking its self
with illicit white snow and angels of dust
trickled on happy strokes of promiscuous love.
Tainted memories flooded the corridors of home
eyeing through my dim potted dome
I trusted the lies and rode them into hell daring
the fury of their fire to ignite me into a haunting
blaze
Spiraling into the sun

Kingdom

You conquered the dragon,
to save the kingdom,
and rescue the girl.
But you burned your village,
became poor without your gold
I couldn't fall that low to save you ...
or climb that high to find you.
And I couldn't save you
when you fell off your dragon
and in to the sea.
And asked me to be less
than I wanted to be..
you were my favourite nightmare,
my fire that frightened the night

but I don't miss trying
To swim over your tides
or save myself on a cloud in your sky...

Creature

Sweet creature
You tried to drown me....,
Chocolate covered storms, dwindled in the
presence of normal,
something so mundane it spiraled me closer to
the insane
An ethereal hunger so deeply penetrated its
frightening.
awakening in soaked sheets
Ravaged by the emptiness of your absence
Howling like a thousand piecing wolves evoke
the rage in my mind,
a wickedly devilish thoughts comes to mind, you
seek to conquer me.
But I heed you a warning
I know how to enjoy the smell of burnt roses in
the morning,
and the eyes I gazed into longing,
I cover with silk....
dressed in diamonds...
It's pure goat milk ...

Removal of you

Sometimes the understanding of a conclusion is
that it no longer needs you to describe its
end……
Words don't need a plate form to stand on
For I can, with every sense of my bein
Feel that your gone ..

Bound

It grew towards me, this inanimate thing...
And I could feel the world, becoming still
and I. and it….alone,
there we were... surrounded by peace.
A moment in transcendence
It remained,
complacent upon my desire for it to exist,
It never left me... or abandoned me…
Even when my emotions become just too much.
and that is what you should have been!
As opposed to water
So easily disrupted, by the fire burning
underneath it
, I just don't understand,
how you unravel love… in such a way.
that it made it ok for you…. to keep walking
away
This lifeless object, in my immediate
understanding
was capable of far more love for me... then a
man with a beating heart
I can only shrug,
and admit…that the path must keep moving
forward,

and I alone……. will be the carrier of its eternal
stride.
Your barely but a mere thought in the back of
my mind
senseless as it all seems to unstitch itself
as easily as it was built by stone...
forever in complacency
But I fear
we may always
keep walking this way

Fairy Angels

Horror lingers on a wild wind
ships take fairy angels
into your crescent wind
For I lay under a moon of light
And cross my heart,
for one last kiss goodnight

Here I Remain

Simplicity marks its infinite defile
I ache for what propelled my body…
To bend in movements of profound love

The dark road bares no resemblance here
It lacks a familiar face
My heart barren in this empty place
Bleeding in the ditch drawn leaves
You'd left me upon…

I sacrificed my heart
While you moved on….

My tongue lays dormant
As I unfold the layers of your lies
I never knew you … a stature so strong
Would rupture so easily
As the frailty of his human nature
Reveals his weakness

You spawned my moon…
And for that an eternal hunger penetrates me… I
knew you'd aid in my destruction

So I let you hang,
And mount our mark in the remanence
Of what remains

Loved

We stared our eyes
 connecting into points our words not dare
speak, for the sheer magnitude of words was too
much, it would have taken the moment away
from us

All this time...
Lingering.... Longing.....
In a desert of dust